POEMS

Robert B. Des
Dillsburg PA
3 March 2004
4977

POEMS

JOHN POCH

[signature] 4977

Orchises
Washington
2004

Bob,

Keep looking into the
Word &, hopefully, these
words.

Best blessings,

[signature]

Library of Congress Cataloging-in-Publication Data

Poch, John, 1966-
    [Poems. Selections]
    Poems / John Poch.
        p. cm.
    ISBN 1-932535-00-4 (alk. paper)
    I. Title.

PS3616.O28P64 2004
811'.6—dc21

2003056414

ACKNOWLEDGMENTS

These journals first published the following poems—*Agni:* "Keeping"; *Colorado Review:* "Chess"; "Postcard from the Fuss of All Ithaca, Post-Bedpost"; *Communiqué:* "Home Life"; *Hiram Poetry Review:* "The Veery"; *Minnesota Review:* "Moving Next Door"; *The Nation:* "House Finches"; "Migration"; "October Ballad"; *New England Review:* "The Crow Poem"; "The Island"; "The Kite"; "The Oar"; "Yeats and the Right Hand"; *Paris Review:* "The Starlet"; *Passages North:* "Before the Night Flight"; "Expecting"; *Petroglyph:* "Land of Sleep"; "Last Day at the Raptor Center"; "Ode to Beeches in Winter"; *Ploughshares:* "The Owl and the Table"; *Re:generation:* "No Wall"; *Salmagundi:* "October Jogger"; *Sarasota Review:* "Song"; *Seneca Review:* "Blackberries"; *Southwest Review:* "In Defense of the Fall"; *Windhover:* "Toward Port au Prince"; and *Yale Review:* "Aubade."

"Re-Wiring the House" appeared in the program of the 92nd Street Y for the 1998 "Discovery"/*The Nation* Prize. A portion of "Winter Song" appeared on the Collective Soul album, *Dosage* (Atlantic Records, 1999).

Several of these poems appeared in the chapbook, *In Defense of the Fall* (Trilobite Press, 2000).

Blue Mountain Center, The MacDowell Colony, and The Constance Saltonstall Foundation for the Arts provided valuable time and space to write and shape this manuscript. Colgate University awarded me its generous and incomparable Creative Writing Fellowship, for which I am grateful.

Chad Davidson, my careful reader, thank you.

Orchises Press
P. O. Box 20602
Alexandria
Virginia
23200-1602

G 6 E 4 C 2 A

To Meghan

CONTENTS

Let me make a clean breast of it here, and frankly admit that I kept but sorry guard. With the problem of the universe revolving in me, how could I—being left completely to myself at such a thought-engendering altitude,—how could I but lightly hold my obligations to observe all whale-ships' standing orders, "Keep your weather eye open, and sing out every time."

—Herman Melville, *Moby-Dick*

TOWARD PORT AU PRINCE

Away from Barbancourt
we hurry in the long, gray missionary bus.
Two dozen orphans happy with our songs and gifts—
until their clothes are traded for charcoal sticks,
a goat head, a bag of meal, duller clothes.
Seventeen, I'm looking over stony fields
and the passing rows of ragged banana trees.
Haitians file down the road along the drainage ditches
toward a town. But toward nowhere, really,
compared to this wild pace, as if even
our mission bus is fleeing the bankruptcy.
Though the road dust and heat coat us in a dim film,
you give in and rest against me. You sleep.
The air is mixed with diesel, charcoal, and rum.
Open sewers, sweaty Creole translators.
We have a mission and move into the error
that lies before us, unavoidable.
In a moment, a jeep coming the other way
will career off the side of our crowded bus,
and though we will be safe, the jeep will veer
and bounce across the ditch into a small market
where Haitians will be flung like shirts from a drawer.
One woman will die instantly, her body fixed
against the wreckage of a vegetable stand
where eggplants have fallen around her arms—
and the miracle—no one else hurt badly.
The driver of the jeep will scramble through the crowd
to an empty field where he will be caught
and stoned according to some invisible rule
hanging like a dead branch in the fetid air.
My father will not allow the bus to be boarded
or our driver taken. We will withdraw
from the scene and navigate military road blocks
with the usual bribes of cologne and pens.

You will pull yourself against my chest to hear
my heartbeat thud above the questions and prayer.
Tonight, at the hotel, you will tell me you love me,
and we will go down to the courtyard, down
to the dusty chairs at the gate, and eat oranges.
A voodoo priest in a red satin cape,
horns tied to his head with fishing line,
will lead the procession of a hundred revelers
bringing their clatter of sticks, cans, and bells
to a stop on the gravel before the iron gate.
The priest will pass a crude bag at the end of a stick
through an opening in the bars. We won't take it,
I'll speak the name of Jesus to you and to the air,
and they'll go off kicking with their music anyway.
This is how the day will happen, but for now
you are comfortable against me here traveling
in the missionary bus toward Port au Prince
knowing we have done some good this morning.

THE KITE

Port au Prince, 1995

Sewage washes through the streets
with every rain, through bathing ditches
and lepers' culverts into the tropical sea.
Above, a missionary plane makes its exit.

Concerning toys, there are the hoop and stick,
dolls of rags. But mostly, little kites:
some plastic trash tied to frames of little sticks.
Examples hang from frayed and sagging power lines,
decorations on the gates of hell—last delights
of the machete-less Tontons Macoutes.

Pariah dogs in every town
appear at stoops of crooked doorways,
glowering over their ribcages, sullen.
Tomorrow will be five years
the baseball factory stands abandoned.
Dead, too, the doll-clothes industry.

Often at night, Cité Simone, the slum named
for a tyrant's wife, flickers in a power shortage
till the main road's naked bulbs are smothered
and bicycles loaded with sticks clatter into ditches.

This morning, a pot-bellied boy combs
the garbage heap sea on Harry Truman Boulevard
in search of the fabric that will unravel
a string long enough to fly his tiny kite.

I get seasick. My mind becomes
a cake crumb flung by a child
onto a lake after a wedding:
the hungry minnows pick at me.
At a Michigan wedding once,
after kissing and cake, the groom
led the bride by her hand into a boat.
Him in his tux and her in the gown—
I thought they'd drown, at least fall in.
They teetered, happy on the brink.
But he rowed her across, singing
her a tree song, faint and fading
till they stepped out on a stone and waved
to us, symbolically.
Dizzy with wind-raked water, I sat
beneath a pine with a new grief.
A storm was blowing up like a rose.
A lady took me in to where the band
had begun again. I danced
unhappily to a worship tune
passing from aunt to aunt
like a recipe or news from home.
My father was the minister,
and he had left me there till four.
I had no watch. There were no clocks.
I looked toward the double doors.
The bride and groom burst in, the wind
and rain behind them. Her tangled hair,
his rumpled shirt, almost untucked.
They had been running. Water wanted
to drown them, wind to strip from them
the mirror-work of calm love hummed.
For now, they'd won.

          To be lost, gone
under her oyster dress was all
anybody wanted, just laid
in the lace and veil and train, to shine
in death rather than darken.
I walked to the front porch and stood
on the wooden deck. It seemed a prow.
The rain threw diamonds at my shoes.
Then it was coming down in sheets.

TYING THE KNOT

Whether tying on a fine elk hair imitation
while on an island boulder in the middle
of a caddis fly hatch or tugging tight
the knots in twine on a trellis for climbing peas
back at the colony garden, I am happy.
Camping, I tied a couple ropes to trees
and hoisted high a bag of food and trash
to foil the bears and mice and varmint whatnot.
I lucked out unwittingly drawing a knot taut
at the dock, was proud of the way a bow
became a hitch, a cinch I didn't know, keeping
the canoe tethered nicely like a present
for the next mariner. My morning prayers
have been threaded black with worry for verse,
for answers, with knots of a distant piano
drifting through the woods and over the lawn,
those knotted half-notes strung across
a winding and imaginary staff and bars,
making and unmaking the chords and melodies
like Penelope's garment, the keen piano
seeming to say, *Penelope*, weeping and faithful
to the man lashed to a mast coming home,
passing the time, passing the nautical knots,
aching for the song, the story, physically,
knots of the muscles gone wrong in my own neck
and back, knots of Inkan lives bound with the cords
of superstition beyond the Word of truth,
knots of my own religious cowardice
and doubt, yet knots of grace below the mountain
of God. Thou shalt not kill, but live and knot.
A neat knot need not be re-knotted.
Naughty, to steal that line of climbing knots.
A wrong knot in a rope or board or line
of poetry or any other institution

(a wind knot in the tippet, for instance)
can cut the tensile strength in half, yet knots
are charming in a good pine paneled room,
the eyes and mouths of a house, making
up stories on the ceiling, telling legends
in a constellation of countenances.
Tying back into the Inkans, while I am not
a khipu keeper, not the historian
of censuses and crops and sheep and tribute
to the present king all wrapped round my waist
in pendant strings, the two knots in the knitting
of the blue hat you made me begin and end
the knit and purl of a warmer winter story.
Truth is, you have been a long time coming,
captivating with your net of casting on.
The khipu's truth is more than a quantitative account.
It is the quality of life and life
more abundantly tied to the mortal real.
So this morning, my truest tangle, only you
can explain how I woke up with a piece
of white wool yarn wound round itself
beside the bed in a soft pattern I consider,
but can't construe, the strongest form
of affection in contemporary art. A thrill,
when you say, *Yes, of course I will,* unfurls
like a fully rigged nine-knot yawl sail, how fast
we haul, how many knots I've left behind,
how my second life comes on twice as strong.

THE ISLAND

My white island whiling away the hour
down the aisle, I must have shipwrecked
on your shore on purpose. I am done
with travel, a fragile compass come
to a white sand snow-blind prayer.
You and your two palms, the hammock
of your arms between them, hold me here
half-dozing, half composing a poem
of the calmest ocean's greatest tide
withdrawn, leaving lines woven in sand
and marking the land as its own.
Like this I am drawn on, drawn in, and hide
myself in you. Farewell for now to every friend.
Look how the smiles, like a hundred little fish,
flash on fire in a bay of midday light.
Unveil, avow, avail yourself to me, your wish.
Look at me, your shipwrecked book, and write.

They said we were a postcard, facing away
in evening light like that. Beyond us, beyond the day
the cloudbank broke up bleeding over the treetops
like a vanquished dragon, and then the sunset dropped
with its gold vault and shaft spoke haul
already dragged away and spent like a call.
Did we appear to have slain, done battle?

Abandoning the rest who gazed
from the lazy porch with their music and beer,
down the gravel path, we settled for a place
on the grass where no one else could hear.
You said you were taking dragon's blood;
you saved the container. You weren't kidding;
it was there in your purse with the knitting.

The greater cave of night becomes your love
every time. The stars still an hour off,
we were captured in a last trap of light, worth
preserving, sending, held, perhaps echoic
of something puffing beyond the occasion, heroic.

Inland, I'm off with my oar. Write me. We'll cope.
I'll turn our postcard over to this: your penmanship,
my address scribbled on half a cool white square:
and the other half, the haiku-like hope
of one lucky mailbox:
You and I wish you were here.
Near the pond, I saw a fox.
Love, The Fuss, OXOX.

A reflection buckles.
The slam of the door to the jetway
has shaken the whole windowed wall,
and through our second story
all the plane tails worry:
a worried worker on the tarmac
is unaware of his loneliness,
his red clubs for hands.

I sit here at the gate
unwrapping your note
of coded sighs typed on birch bark:
a short list of pet-names
as simple as white quartz stones gathered
from afternoon walks, arranged
on a sill, unremarkable
in almost any other context.
A necklace of rock-candy stones
rubs the notch below a girl's throat
when she stretches to look over her shoulder
toward the couple bickering over yesterday.
Something yesterday.

Hillside neighborhoods spider out under streetlights
lining the roads below a plane
already airborne. I look up.
Those passengers must look down
and see the swimming pools
lit through like aquamarine,
and the emerald
of a high school baseball diamond,
small, maybe extinguished suddenly
because it's late and the game's over.

Flipping that switch, another lonely figure
moves through the dark,
but happy toward home and sleep.
A woman calls us for boarding. There's no hurry.
What pet-names would make your eyes shine,
what lustrous lights sharply laid
on departure's jet-black tarmac?
For starters, Far Fire.

SNOWSHOEING

We were thirsty. Here, in the snowfall
days later on the quarry floor
the wind churns and the branches,
like the poor arms of desert prophets
whose tongues have long been cut out, shake.
The snow rises up through them
and falls again—sighs of an old
exhausted quarry. What good is this?
What good would it do to climb the hill
and look down on where I stand in the flurries?
I snowshoe away through bare woods
till I stumble through a thin branch silence
into an open meadow of white.

A red fox trotted into our headlights
last week when we rose over the hill
before my house. We slowed to the time
of a snowglobe. He kept in front of us
for thirty yards then disappeared
into the child-size red pines
at the ditch edge. Our eyes. We were
thirsty for more fox. An insult,
I thought, that the sly mind
had already forgotten us while we went on
about the tail, the gait, the sharp mouth
perfect for birds, the face that wedged
so quickly into its bittersweet thicket,
that it need not remember much.

I keep looking down on myself
from a high place, a winter branch,
a ledge of rock and ice and God.

I think the fox is thirsty now,
waking in his winter den below
a pile of felled pines at the quarry.
How his shadow leaned
before him in the headlight glare
while the snow screwed itself down
onto the earth that night of no wind
when the quarry was only a place
I'd heard about, larger in my mind,
deeper, holding water, not full
of spindly ash and beech and birch
and the fox-den pine-pile. If when he turned,
he caught, through the side window
the spark in my eye that prophesied
my snowdrift worry at the quarry,
my waiting above the meadow where
the stream has not quite frozen over,
if he comes and drinks, he celebrates
you, only without memory.

MIGRATION

Are you hiding in a book? I want to read it.
Like Pieter de Hooch's love of the half-open shutter,
you sip your glass of water in the shadow of your bangs,
in the shadow of your book, a judgment
against the fact that every decade is arrogant.
You are so clean you daydream of sheets,
telling no one. Your hands are two magic birds:
one for granting great geographical knowledge and one
for plunging in and out of streams
to stymie your enemies. If these wings come together
in the form of prayer, a nest, or a cup of air,
certain houses and neighborhoods will explode.
Let them come together in the small of my back.

contemporary of
Van Meer

SOLSTICE

What shall I sing?
Sing me about creation.
—Caedmon

Woman of morning brook fluorescence almost unknown,
you save the forty hinges from the doors of a broken home
to build another art. At your shimmering birth, four gentlemen
bowed down at your step into the world: plum, chrysanthemum,
bamboo, and orchid. Anteroom and tearoom are temple
enough for you. Your maker spends half the day, hand-simple,
fastening wood and stone, half the day caring for tools.
Aesthetes say the transfer of wool on a spinning wheel's white spools
is the best example of your sexy metaphysics. The smell of wheat:
of cash and glue and unlaid tile is the healthy wealth you breathe
on me. When you are nothing, you are still the vacation after
the vacation, your tan repose divining future fire behavior.
From a tiny arrangement of forget-me-not you derive
a joy like finding in an unknown monk's marginalia a whole life.
According to the increased timbre of your humming,
home of the fighting jackrabbits, your day is coming!

SONG

Now, there is a fine vine fire blue
green illusion in your arms
no couturier could deal,
no dress on a door could adorn,
a deliberate witchery of rhythm
in your sobbing. I want to be you,
and your cheek against my chest.
I am.

I mean, yesterday
I was something else insignificant
like a chipped stack of black dishes.
Let some yard sale be done with them,
or send them to a tornadoed town.
Arrange them at the foot of a broken oak
with napkins and faux-fruit.

Are you one of the gods, girl?
With your prehensile style of loving,
you are the reason for groves.
There is no child in you, yet.
Let me say I will clothe the prairie
with a tablecloth of praise.
Bring nothing. Bring nothing.

If she faints while in her fast, the chef awaits
her word in a kitchen hidden at the heart
of the hotel. Her hunger, his counterpart,
lightens the gourmet boredom this dinner shift,
and he will pass word on to others if
she keeps her promise or she abrogates.

For now, assistants make the kitchen wild
with shifting pans among the ovens, stoves,
and countertops. The fires leap like loves
that heat beloved flesh and flicker there.
Half a cup of millet has been prepared
so she can break her fast on something mild.

He thinks she practices the next day's scenes
pacing the room some thirty stories up.
He wants to be, if she should choose to stop,
the man who comforts her and makes her laugh.
Or if she still desire, the imagined chef
who makes the pretty food in magazines.

He's conscious of his lousy chef costume.
Ignoring her who hungers over town
is difficult when evening rush dies down
to tinkling trays of silverware and plates
the busboys balance. The wine concatenates
the patrons' voices in the dining room

into a buzz of lavish adulations
for some of the finest dinner fare they've had
in years. They want to see him in his hat
and checkered pants. And for dessert, they wish
he'd light the room with a flaming brandy dish.
Somewhere she asks for nothing but his patience.

The dance next door with a dumbbell full of sand.
The girl across the lawn holds, in her hand,
suspended time. Her parents plant a tree.
Small shoulders pull against the gravity.
Her heavy dance: a shadow-laden reader
new to the window tax repeal, sun-feeder.
The neighbors hear her reeling—she hellos
goodbyes and leans back like the humming cellos.

Cleaning the windows makes me feel like a god.
The scene out there is over when my breath
fuzzes. I roam the house to clean, feel odd.
O mirror, soldier full of holes, the spray
I spray on me, a candidate for death.
My teeth are stones around a flame I say.

HOUSE FINCHES

To watch the pair of house finches
that frequent the neighbor's feeder,
I leave the charcoal blinds pulled up.
The berry-splashed chest of the male—
each morning—makes me pause.
He flits away when full, or troubled
by the cat behind the window pane.
But he's back again within the hour.
Evenings, we owe our different debts
to the woman who fills the feeder tray,
who also chooses open blinds
and wanders room to room, past
the long blue light of the aquarium.
(She caught me watching yesterday.)
The fish, from here, are almost still,
a drifting string of colored lights.
Her boyfriend's echoes of her name
reverberate and scare the cat;
bird seed scatters with the flight
of startled finches. Sunflower seeds,
far from the flower they once composed,
lie like black collapsed stars.

The Oar

"The Devil knows how to row."
—Coleridge

I have cheated at everything. When I lived in town
behind a park-side house on the river, I'd lie
in my hammock with a woman, my arm slung down
over the side like an oar tired of rowing.
After so much swaying, I'd talk about the sky.

My voice was getting even lower then: words fell
randomly grand as green-gone-bleeding maple leaves.
Suspicious of my luck, I thought to cheat myself
on the side. Likable and older, tired of rowing,
I made unlikely wagers with friends and thieves.

I couldn't lose. I bought, in a bow-tied haranguing
at the rainy train-station, a little painted scene
of a house that smacked of home. A brown umbrella hanging
at my side dripped like an old oar I was tired of rowing.
The picture warmed me, and it was from a magazine.

A broken arm from a fall one night—I hoped I was even.
A woman brought a saffron dish to my house near the park.
It's like eating perfume, I said. *It's good to have heaven
on your side*. Like Odysseus retired from rowing,
like Homer far removed, I told some stories in the dark.

BLACKBERRIES

In the blackberry patch, a wren burst
from thorns to a sideways, swaying perch
on the sumac. Sue me, I said. His baiting me
away wasn't working, as I was out
not for wren eggs but blackberries.
It backfired—his raspy whistle—
making me want what was worth
the instinctual trick. Maybe a wren chick
instead of an ice cream topping.
Stopping was not an option, now,
not for the curious. He was furious
I didn't follow him, or I was projecting
something about a lover's phone fight
onto nature. I hate your guts, you didn't say,
but I felt that way for a second, and a walk
to clear my head seemed right (you see,
I fled a dark sorrow) among the brambles,
imaginary nests or not. The wren forgot me
farther down the brambled path
with my stained hands and forgetfulness.
Which is forgiveness with a toll.

HOME LIFE

"Tell me, tongue of fire..."
—James Merrill

I loved a house and it burned down.
The sun rolled over the scene,
proud and showing the fire off.
My birthday, and in the rubble
the candle-fires sang, *You wish.*
Men watched, and their stories made
the other summers brighter.

The sirens conspired,
and the dogs in chorus.
Help brought the curtains on,
and the darkness was no better.
Final was the leaving of machines,
the secret puffs of smoke.
Who's there?

My sunken ship, my darkened heels,
my black ties dripping,
fallen from hanging themselves.
The nurse says the physician says,
If the darkness returns (be bright),
come in, we'll have a look.

What burned was the house.
It was always burning, its windows open
asking for the wind's bright eyes.

No Wall

"She dreamed she saw the lion sharpen his claw."
                                        —Donald Justice

The noon's eclipse was not the only omen.
Out of the east, a ripping like a saw
pushed once, a ragged breath, a lion claw
tearing the veil that separated common
from consecrated. Neither man nor woman
could sew it back. Its downfall seemed a flaw.
Wood groaned but held as if in rigid awe
of weight and a wet soaking in. So human—
to ask what caused the small quake after all,
for who could tell what things would happen?
The daylight saw no seraphim unfurled,
no singing stones or trees in praise; no wall
lay fallen. Dead at last, he hung there, open
as one who would be buried in the world.

THE VEERY

I.

I have predicted the end of spring for the fifth time,
and here are the low clouds scudding in cold
from the north again, dissolving at the edges
while reassembling themselves from within.
Like memory in old age, they are not the shape
of anything. They ride—white thoughts
of little consequence, little rebellions—
a lavish blue heaven of all knowledge.
The meadow shadows come toward me
like a cash register opening. Cold cash.
The clouds do not want to disappear.
This middle ground of insistent mystery reads,
like Braille, the real world of scattered buttercups
shuffling through the green. I am so close.
A dragonfly alights, pulses, fat on mosquitoes,
tips over his stalk, happy the cold has slowed
his dying. Spring is dying, stubbornly.

II.

Last night, a woman read aloud her story of another woman,
sorrowful, having to make due with her quixotic,
faithless man. It swooned in the telling half the time.
She was enraptured in her pages and couldn't know,
caught up in her voice that seemed to come
from outside herself far away—a spotlight or two
through smoke—baptizing her. You could be happy
for her, yet lost enough to fall away toward
the real room, watching the pretty secret of two painters
told in a shared smile, his hand absently moving
over the back of his own neck, her toes arching
to the remembered pleasure of their afternoon.
Others sighed as if imagining their own tombstones.

But then, a veery began her singing from deep
in the woods beyond the screened-in porch.
I thought, God, spring has overflowed into summer.
What do you want from me, a gossip, a liar
taking the hand of truth? With the music
of the veery like a thin syrup poured into
the bird's thin flute throat rather than out,
like some video-game-pretend-end, He said,
You couldn't bear it if you knew the final score. Sudden
death. The story was over and everyone clapped.
I started home alone saying, *I will try to bear it
anyway,* and the veery began again
from some different place; hidden high
in the last shadows, she seemed to follow me.
Such fidelity, I thought summer had come.

Always calling, *Fall*
on me,
three o'clock black
little shadow flat
as the water at
the bottom of a well,
I fell from a wall
to fill a floor. I feel.
No matter that
I'm crushed by a little girl
named Ella or an elephant.
Like a right-hand
thin candle-spill,
I love the formal
lonely lull of tall
followers. Done,
no longer
mistaken for one.
Love, encompass, feast
full, fall southeast
on me. Understand. I will lead you.

KEEPING

When I was nine, a neighbor passed away
and left us stacks of beehives only to be stored
in our barn long empty of its cows and hay.
Our fields lay fallow—we were under other orders.
It was a ruined milk farm, and we brought
to this failure our gaping childish sight
soaking up hope's color like maple leaves.
Our prayers lifted a bouquet of absence in dawnlight
and foggy shattered petals settled in the trees
by evening over streams that wound down
to another county, blessed someone, we thought.
Still, each beehive was only a bare cupboard
of mouse leavings and bat splatter. Rot
was not far off as the white wood grayed.
Like a patient saint, someone could have covered
himself in white. Someone could have conveyed
just one white box to the orchard. But no priestly ghost
of smoke would bring the grave and stately swarm
who eat and worship blossoming. Unfair.
Imagine there is a limb's hive heart here almost
singing. My wife, I raise this arm, its warm
hollow is yours. It will receive you, I swear.

EXPECTING

The cattails nodding above the marsh in autumn breeze
fluff at the edges like buffalo fur. This is the ease
with which the prim girl says of the pregnant farmer's daughter,
She let herself go. This round loneliness, this tatter
whitest on the hem of cotton light must be open
to gossip, pitying the truth inside it, hoping
the red-wing blackbird will make a cattail metronome
to a music of evening wind, knowing chickadees come
to line their winter nests with the down of failure's bed.
Think of the daughter standing in a doorway, her head
against the frame, her hair in tangles across her face,
fire light in the strands' inadequate embrace.

WINTER SONG

"At Christmas—dead time of the year—
When wolves eat wind, and nothing more"

—Villon

I walk down to the lake. While the cold is shocking,
a peace descends in gusts and somersaults
through reeds—the hiss and whistle interlocking.

Tonight the sky's a dozen layered cobalts
awash with flecks of God and angels talking
over whether you're mine. So nearly salts

are stars that melt the cold of space, unlocking
warmth like footsteps in a solitary waltz.
Along the shore, I count the threes while walking

the sidewalk home. I pass the darkened vaults
of late doorways as if I were a king.
Like this, I chain a whisper to my faults.

Too dreamy, the long line of peachleaf willows,
their leafless branches making a haze of orange
over the asphalt walkway cleared of snow and salted.
The wide plate glass high in the library frames the scene
of the latest sleet coming in curtains over Broad Street.
The groundsmen raise their brows. Winter has been known
to pelt the general respect into things. Students, indoors,
force themselves up little ladders before brown mountains
of books or toward dictionary stands. The longest word
is last night's blizzard's cursive crest of the snowbank
blown high along the south meadow where I live
clear down to Hoose Road. No one has the patience
to decipher the long-winded scrawl or mouth the syllables.
(A kind of drawn-out almost-whistle.) Maybe
the beeches who rattle their fits of leaves at winter
all winter, scratching back, could comprehend it.
The beeches hold those long-dead leaves as testimony
to the sunlight before the first snow five months ago
until the hour an hour-steady breeze unlatches spring
like a little white gate thrown open to green.
Then the beeches let go, make more.

When I carry the mirror in my hands
through the house of disarray, arms extended,
dirty-shirted, I am a sailboat of bones
blown with the smoke from Mexico forest fires
drifted all the way to Oklahoma.
I see through me like a slough.
There are dishes. Hallway art.
Outside the stairwell, a lawn and sky bobbing.
In the kitchen of the latest life,
my chairs and table alone are the furniture of worship,
carried off at my turning. Clocks turn
back in mirrors. I put the mirror down.

I knew a woman, the wind smoothed her out.
Small silver birds were in her ears:
she read me like an open jalousie.
She touched the keys when she called me martyr.
She left, her hair behind her swaying.
I saw the fins of divers kicking from a wreck.

Well, the mirror is upon me. I loom.
What will they say when I become a proverb?
That was his best Narcissus? When dying,
he could outskeleton the bugs? Laughter.
He loved the number one. Mirrors slow us down,
but make for bigger rooms.

October Ballad

There goes the mission summer.
Yoke us up the sun.
Go start the harvest tractor
we built from skeletons.

The scapulas are fenders,
the pelvis is a seat.
A humerus for shifting
the gears beneath our feet.

Young blackbirds kick from bushes
the hummingbirds' gray nest.
They shriek like falling glasses
to pieces and molest.

The last potatoes hidden,
they'd rather rot than see.
Does daylight vision threaten
this dirt-blind manatee?

Insouciant sari gauzes
of warmer winds blow wide
to the naked arms of losses,
outstretched, crucified.

The monarchs growing old are
only passing through.
They lug black bones on shoulders,
on fire, to Mexico.

Our mothers gather children
around their skirts in rings
of blameless leaf tornadoes—
small Elijahs—II Kings.

Job's job was really losing.
Our father's—to clear-cut worth
and ride death; eulogizing,
lowering the ear to earth.

To praise it all, arranging
bowls of inedible gourds
with colored corn for strangers,
come giving in death's doors.

Kierkegaard would frown at my longing for her ponytails
alive with love. No race, her patient autumn rhythm spells
the turning of the leaves. I'm driving, storebound, out of fruit,
and she seems a cornucopia to me. All peaches and pears,
her yield demands the others stop. She jogs her warm-up suit
around a Studebaker, its back seat a love bench, threadbare.
Like that, I'm past. I leave her in exhaust,
the rear view disappearing till all is lost.

Regina, my heart's a liquor-spill. Run, reign, fell
a family tree, but leave alone an island where bread
is the yeastless cracker of exile and a new Bible smell
rises after every rain. The first freeze of fall, and a fear
drops in me. Like my pen when I drift off in a chair,
it wakes me up and rights me toward a better bed.

RE-WIRING THE HOUSE

The gutted wire in piles out back like old snakes,
killed to keep us safe, will be hauled away and sold.
Each day some small part of the house is dead
for a while. I learn to do without or have to hold
a book to window light. In time, lost time is found

or overshadowed. With light. With safety. No fraying wire
igniting blossoms of flame within the plastered lath,
no lost power later. There is marred nostalgia
in the temporary mess and loss, although each room will have
a coruscating angel of a ceiling fan.

I know what's in the attic—the stifling dark.
Itself stifled. Today the workers crawled above
like animals of thought in a troubled mind.
The whole house was a head: the door—a mouth,
the windows—eyes, the porch rail—teeth.

The body underground and buried to the neck?
We see how Dante's idle giants towered down.
After the evening news, I walk outside to pray
some scattered notes of what I have or haven't done
in a light that's halfway finished, charged with warmth.

Two sawhorse shadows lean across the front lawn air,
portraying how our names will fall from anybody
they are. Like spills they stretch and run away,
now toward the neighbor's trees, assuming bodies,
then are lost. So we are lost in thought again.

AUBADE

The sun on the thin beige blinds gives shape to
the little house-finch silhouette, in lieu
of the house finch that comes each day on cue.
A momentary tottering tattoo
held on a skin of light. A visual echo.
An unreal film. Before she flits to go
to her mate, I watch the bobbing shadow slow
till stationary on the blinds. We know,

in Iowa in midday half-light, you
made (with paper and a pin-prick O
and the eclipse) a smile, a crescent—although
it wasn't the moon that lit the walk below,
that lost its shape in the widening, fading glow;
it was the sun that disappointed and grew.

FASTING

You hear the forecast minus four
coming in pine hush and unhush
in the windchimes, and indoors
the ladybugs love how you crank the heat.
Somewhere, they hatch. A few wild spirals
around the lamp and they crash like commas
on the page, their tissue underwings pulled in
until they achieve the period's full-stop.
It's winter and they are unlucky in a lack
of aphids. Within a day, having strolled
the windowsills, the ladybugs
ossify, as brutally useless and barren
as abandoned helmets, dark orange
and black shells with a little white warpaint
smeared high across the face guard.
A fitted sheet of fear is in the minus four.
You went back to bed this morning
praying you could praise on paper.
The ladybugs swarmed the bulb above
and crawled across the flawless ceiling,
a poem of punctuation only.
It's time for fasting. Like a dictionary,
you keep to yourself the luck of comma
after comma, hide in prayer fragments,
cold among tiny fires, tugging
at your own tissue black beneath the shell.

Mostly the birds I'd seen before: peregrine,
buzzard and vulture, red-tailed hawk. And then
the smaller pair of sparrow hawks. DANGER,
the signs said. Owls, small to tall, stranger
in the different ways that they were wise.
One had a scar for one of his amber eyes.
The birds were here only if in peril—
the osprey struck by a poacher's arrow.

Through the open downhill butterfly walk—
not even a moth. We waited half an hour
on a bench graffitied with the latest love talk,
saw little or nothing in the empty flowers.

We saved for last two eagles, caged
in a crate no larger than our living room.
The golden eagle clenched, stern in her place.
Across the perch the bald eagle raged,
ailing with his mangled wing since June.
How bright his anger stared through the doomed
pale-yellow eyes. He neither looked for help,
nor to refuge beyond his injured self.
We looked away. To strewn feathers and beaks
of chickens bloody with flies, to the white streaks
of feces on the wall behind the perches.
His sudden screeches seemed to curse us.
Back to the car. Even then we could hear.
You said some day you'd like to volunteer,
to give more of yourself, but you couldn't
find a way to get out there. You didn't.

Our bodies steam in the cold humid evening.
We stand around a pine and watch the owl
halfway up blink her gold displeasure
down on our hollow mocking vowels.
Nothing here is like you: your presence
has come as if ropes pulled on my breathing.

I want to know what makes us grow quiet
as clothes can be, what makes me wish for a stick
or little stone to make the owl fly, yet
what holds me—watching the animal above—
from cruelty. We're cruel, though. And sick
wanting it to go; we're sick of love.

Each face tilted in air—we are not waiting
for a familiar song to start, or a kiss.
When she goes we are left translating,
and there is no name for our beautiful loss.
There is a name for how we turn for home
and forget this moment. It is your name.

The cedar shakes at evening took on
an Edward Hopper glow, broken
with the hard-edge shadows he made
famous in paint. These shadows fled
because of the hill a half-mile west.
Shooting hoops was perfect: when I missed,
sometimes, the ball careened toward
the house, its downward sloping yard.
Retrieving the ball, I'd pause, stand stunned
at each new lack of light and want
to miss this way again. I did,
and further, into the flower bed
against the house, but not on purpose.
It was there I heard the scratching, nervous,
coffin-trapped, from under the shakes.
I guessed a bat when I heard the shrieks
stretching from some daydream trauma.
I was sure when I saw the guano
in the bed below. I sat in the grass
and waited, watched the little claws
reaching out between the shakes,
then back in, not ready to wake.
A different kind of cave and dark
(out of de Chirico's early work)
poured over the scene as when one dreams
and wakes, slowly, and swallows the dream.

No neighbors, but if there were, they'd think—
Affected poet, worshipping
his house! He ought to mow the lawn.
A quick look toward the high hill—gone
the pinks and oranges of before,
gone the long cloud-edge of fire.
Now the eyes must adjust, or ears
take over, yet I strained for fear

I wouldn't clearly catch him catch
the air; his claws shimmied the edge
of the shake, a wing struggling, his body
must have been disjointed and putty-
soft to fit. I blinked. He dropped
like that and caught the dark with soft
skin wings thin as human eyelids.
Another scrambled down and fled,
and then eight more. I watched them pivot
about the yard about a minute,
another shadow coming on,
the full moon cold and low and strong.

THE CROW POEM

The crows brought black awkward rips to bear
on the day, strutting through the low meadows
their imperious plague, their blue-black flu glare—
and then their blacker breath of wings
lifting into the lowest branches of the pines
where they waited for my heart to explode
and no one to come. So they could come.
I hated them for nothing. I wanted a crow poem.
Gossips interrupted by their subject, they let the room
of the woods go quiet as I passed. They rowed
higher into the rafters, peered out over ledges.
Meanwhile, peonies are content with the black ant feet
circling, touching, prodding, circling the edges
of their petals as a blind old woman might learn
the face of a boy who bears her name forward
into the world on his countenance. A boy, sweet
with a milk smell on his skin, who recalls for her
the Easter service, and she coaxes him, listens
to the petals of his lips tell the story.
I was that boy, believing He is risen,
and I need again the feminine vision,
for the peony will open, white with religion,
ants fallen—like soldiers around the tomb.
So I shall be content with crows as I was
content walking home last night, a moth
at the throat, a damp-winged luna moth
who thought my throat a moon, a warm home
in a dark wood. This is the crow poem,
I thought, clutching and frantic on me,
ironic with white and soft green wingblow
climbing up my chin, off and leaving me,
dark as if inside a sleeping crow.

LAND OF SLEEP

written in upstate NY
She dies in Fla of cancer

These are days I worry about the well.
I walk the property dusty-shoed, shoddy, arriving
at the pond cracked and shadowed at the outer shell
like an antique mixing bowl abandoned at evening.
The singing I make is nervous on the hillside,
my tongue soaking up half the sound my throat
wants out, calling rain from over the hill
beyond this hill. I sing anyway until a car comes up the drive
lifting a storm of dust that drifts and coats
the trees as if it were a prescient dream of death.

Driving once, I saw a sign: *Land of Sleep*. Mattresses.
I had been at the hospice holding the hand of my friend
dying in Florida. I was driving back from swimming
in the gulf on a break from our watch.
A bald eagle banked and pitched across
the four lane road and up into a tree.
In the car next to me, a couple my age didn't see.
I wanted them to see it. They were discussing something
inane. Though maybe they had someone dying, too.
I thought, she's gone and this eagle is the sign.
Then *Land of Sleep* above the other strip-mall signs.
I felt sure she had died while I was swimming,
but she was still breathing. Is it mean to say
it was disappointing either way? Back at the hospice
she was a skeleton almost. Unconscious
as when I had arrived three days before.
And there were two more days to go.
I kept on singing hymns to her.
She went a week with no water. I felt ashamed, lost
when sleep came in waves, when I washed.
There are days the Psalms mean more.

In this antique mirror with beveled edges
the backward upside-down handwriting fills
the emptiness like an upstart algae high
on too much oxygen. The tide goes left
as if I float that way above it, adrift
on a minor kingdom, looking for a fish,
then catching my reflection, my eyes.
I'm curious about our vanity.
If I look up I'm stuck. Stuck up. I knew
this woman, when she walked into a room
that had a mirror and stood or sat nearby
facing it, she'd say, *How convenient!*
She was so beautiful everyone forgave her.
Small doll nose, eyes dark, lips dark, dark black hair
that, when she swam and rose up, smoothed out
back and over her shoulders—an oil spill
like a ship had sunk hours ago and forgotten
itself. She dated Arabs, rich from diamonds.
They gave her cars and phones but she came to swim
in our apartment pool. She was my sister's friend.
I delivered pizzas weekends, cursing my hat.
Once, she took us out, my sister and me,
on the Arab credit card. At the restaurant,
she intimidated waiters by looking right
at them. She faced me, the mirror behind my head.
It's one thing when a mirror is in front of me...
How convenient. I have never recovered from that.
She found a husband who would beat her up.
It makes me think of mirrors breaking. Crystal,
this look. No prophecy, but memory.

The crystal windchimes call me out to see,
but I will show them and make a like tune
for the ground strewn red with leaves
reeking and wet with tree failure, a song

I once heard played on Thomas Jefferson's
crystal set of glasses. Two hundred years
after he'd touched them into melody,
some woman in museum uniform
played an orphan-girl's concerto for us,
Vivaldi, fall, a ringing end hanging on,
for me and my sister. But the velvet box
was empty in some spots. She complained
her range was limited. I see my eyes
are wet, but why? It's not that I pity them,
the woman, my sister, the dark girl. My hand
is one veil, the antique mirror another—
its streaks of metal wash behind the glass
decayed with time. It's that I thirst and refuse
to get up from this desk and mirror, pour
myself a glass of water, and drink. Perverse
and unheroic thirst for artifice.

What God hates first. Mirror, mirror,
everyone forgave her because they wanted
to see her rising from that pool, the water
weighing back black hair, her eyes and mouth
more open now with air, and darkness, yes,
but air all velvet, empty, warm, and wet
speaking, *I am the absent glass. You thirst
for me as if I were behind your eyes.*

The owl said, my son, Oak Table,
your stand is strong. I have four talons on each leg,
and you four talons on each leg.
Our cold heavy hold holds mostly air. We are able.
The table did not speak.

We both make our home in the oak.
My eyes glow with the glow of polished oak.
Your grain is feathered smooth beneath the maker's plane.
You shine with polyurethane.
The table did not speak.

Men come to us with hunger and questions
about death. They seat themselves below us.
The table did not speak.

Yet I might trade with one of them one hour
to know the princess' hair, her skin, the thirsty trail
of flattened grass along her paths. Who made her?
Go ask your sister, the book. Your mother, the lake.
The table did not speak.

At dark, looking for the princess and her recipes
of sexy scenes, we find our places in the night
the mice have never known
and move upon the wet wind when no one sees.
But I am tired. I'm tired of morning light.

The table groaned, I am not your son.
I am not even an oak table. I am the altar of God.
And even the princess, even you must come
to bow with me on the soft moss. The owl did not speak,
but turned his head toward the question in his beak.

DEATH

When I was born, everybody died.
I never make my bed, and someone's always
coming behind me, picking up.
I'm a leader.
I lost my keys to a tomb at noon.
My footprint is a single black feather
or a petal fallen from anything (pick a color).
A lover of formality, I'm black and white.
Black tie, barefoot and sloppy.
When I'm on fire, I'm cold.
The broken-legged Lippizaner in a ditch complains my name.
I'm as slow as a spent bullet.
I fear the mirror only.
Bright tattoos of unremarkable people decorate my calves,
and I strut down the beach like a famous wrestler
who has practiced and practiced falling.
Photography is my bag.
I like hiding under the black cloth
while everyone waits for an explosion.
Prayer to my sinews is my idea of fun.
I lie down as much as possible
in a nest of bones till I feel guilty enough
to get up and write an epitaph.
I rhyme with breath.
Everything my father did was a joke.
My mother is a flute, a fluke.
I have wanted to marry Love for so long.
She won't have me.
When I die, everyone will live forever.

THIEF

Before the snow, I stand in a darkening field.
The milkweed of fall, like a city appalled at night,
take flight. The thinnest parachutists
leap past me, a bigger building being built,
no lights yet, so much undone, the new nudist,
a gasoline pump in shadow: miles inside.

When sparrows starve in winter, doors
across the countryside are coaxed open
by their tiny, shining, hematite-eyed prayers.
Bundled up, bread-handed, fortune shines back.
I look for cold because her breath could spin
a nail into blue yarn, so white is the milk of it.

The season holds on like a possession.
Stained glass puddles around me like a shell
melted and thinking of the fall of a color
television, memory gone to snow.
The night sneaks down the hill with its oil coat.
Inside the lining, a blunt metal confession.

Prometheus and his old hawk, sore,
they talk sometimes about the fire,
the broken rule, the broken fence
of his ribs like firewood, recompense
for turning night to day before
the day should be, the taste of flesh,
both raw and cooked, rotten and fresh.
The romance in a candle light.

The hawk is being punished, too:
for taking doves out of the blue
rather than what had fallen.
Wondering how flames make flight,
Prometheus and hawk fall solemn.

Then they make a music of their pain:
the wing-beat wind, the rock, the chain,
the mercy cry of broken host
in concert with the torturer's roar,
his hunger's sterile and nestless brood.
They rival sirens from the coast.
Pretty from a long way off, be sure:
someone's in trouble the color of blood.

WHY I JUST DROPPED THE NATURE BOUQUET

Like a cocoon full of its writhing moth,
at the park's edge, lying beneath a tree
a couple struggles almost secretly
within the thin white sheet they have brought.
Daylight still and nearly home from my walk
around this summer-baked Lubbock lake
bubbling with methane gas or maybe
catfish gasps, I am close enough to see
she is on top. In the fingers of one hand
I hold what I've found: a dove feather,
several sprigs of curly willow. And
a butterfly wing. Nothing in the other.
She must think me strange. She sees
I see. Where are the police,
neither of us will say. She softly sighs
something to the man below, but he won't
look over. He is hardly there, his eyes
must be rolled back so far in his mind
dissolving like pills. In assent,
he only nods he mustn't, for a moment,
move or breathe. Silly me, I want
to comfort her. I am close enough to tell
that two wisps of her hair are falling spent
over them like long dark tassels of a veil.
We are all close to something here.
For a moment, I roll my eyes upward
like him, but not as deep into the sky.
They are waiting for me to disappear.
I am looking away, but I can't look away.
Who looks away at the end of the world?

YEATS AND THE RIGHT HAND

If I make my eyes the calmest almonds,
this ashen lamp-lit hand becomes as Milton's,
a god. The fist, cool stone and molten core:
I labor over holding edges ripe for war.
Armor-bearer brother of the tongues,

what is on your left will meet with death
a hundred times today and depart
with no agreement. Dumb size-of-a-heart
before me, pound the hollow breath
of a dead drum and call the clear-eyed guard.

The knuckles' turret circumscribes a rose
of intimate maroon. Four story tower,
open the palm to praise the light. Flower,
then hold the pen to loose ink like a voice.
A line beyond the mansion darkness knows.

But let us put the dying game away
for good, as deer leave a dew-soaked clearing
at the first hint of light, disappearing
into the closest woods. The sturdy day
will drown the world in another hush as they,
with star-worn faces, change their loves. Not fearing.
They veer their steps around fall leaves, steering
as gold threads hold the reddest cloisonné.

Let us adopt a child; or take our failure
and touch each other's sorry guard, forsaking
pleasure boats. As love avails our leaning
toward rest, the pieces forfeit half their meaning:
what represents our difference, our making
losses come. What's left can love the killer.

How the sap drains back down the trunk
to keep from freezing in the branches.
How the trees are humbled, stripped bare,
and dirt now gets its turn.
How this time of year creation clambers
down to listen to the passing earth.
And the daylight in its quicker southern path.
How we should think of death to keep us calm.

Donne and others married love and death.
The little sparrows with their stuck waxy smiles
gather blessings near the benches,
flitting from perch to ground.
They are mostly mute, diminished
to wings going *finished finished finished.*

teacher Texas Tech
miss. family who were in Haiti